SECRETS
OF THE ZODIAC

SECRETS
OF THE ZODIAC

JANE LYLE

STUDIO EDITIONS
LONDON

Frontispiece:
The Twelve Divisions of the Zodiac — believed to have
been established by the first millenium BC. However,
Taurus and Leo are thought to date from as early as 3500
BC. (Early medieval manuscript)

This edition published 1993 by
Studio Editions Ltd
Princess House, 50 Eastcastle Street
London, W1N 7AP, England

Copyright © Studio Editions Ltd, 1993

Designed by Michael R Carter
Printed and bound in Singapore

ISBN 1 85891 006 4

INTRODUCTION

The Ram, the Bull, the Heavenly Twins,
And next the Crab the Lion shines,
The Virgin and the Scales,
The Scorpion, Archer, and Sea Goat,
The Man that bears the Watering Pot,
The Fish with glittering tails.

TRADITIONAL RHYME

For thousands of years human beings have studied the stars. Sailors and travellers used the pole star to guide them; kings, queens and popes patronized court astrologers; while Venus, the morning and evening star, set the boundaries between dawn and dusk.

Ancient astrologers worked with a system of five planets (Mercury, Venus, Mars, Jupiter and Saturn) plus the Sun and Moon, which were poetically known as the 'luminaries'. The discovery of three 'outer planets' much later – Uranus in 1781, Neptune in 1846 and Pluto in 1930 – expanded and refined astrological knowledge. The 'new' planets were allocated to their proper signs which retained the planet they had originally been given. Hence three signs, Scorpio (Mars and Pluto), Aquarius (Saturn and Uranus) and Pisces (Jupiter and Neptune) have two planets each.

The Anatomy of Man and Woman, shows the astrological associations with the different parts of the body. (*The Très Riches Heures* of the Duc de Berry)

Each planet is said to 'rule' a sign, but since there are currently only ten bodies available, four signs still share one ruling planet – Taurus and Libra have Venus, while Gemini and Virgo have Mercury. It is important to realize that, until the early eighteenth century, astronomers and astrologers were one and the same. Great scientists such as Sir Isaac Newton and Galileo were as familiar with the mechanics of the horoscope as they were with the stars. night sky.

Over the course of centuries, the planets came to represent certain qualities, and were linked to a vast and intricate array of correspondences which included gems, parts of the body, plants and colours. Although these may seem like a ragbag of superstitious nonsense, they represent an attempt to create order and meaning out of chaos, Each sign, its attributes and associated affinities, was intended to symbolize part of the vast pattern of life itself.

The long history of astrology is richly studded with exotic figures, from Babylonian priests to the media stars of today. Its current rise in popularity dates from the nineteenth century, and shows no sign of abating. Popular astrology deals with 'Sun signs' – that is, the sign the Sun was passing through during the month of

Following page
The Celestial Sky. This chart shows the northern and southern hemispheres with the constellations for each sign. The zodiacal constellations provide a backdrop against which we can track the movements of the sun, moon and planets and chart the progress of the year. (Frederick de Wit, 1680)

birth. Each sign has a set of typical characteristics which are closely linked to the traits attributed to its ruling planet, and element.

Understanding your elemental group is the first step towards understanding your Sun sign. Each group shares certain strengths and weaknesses in common. The Fire signs (Aries, Leo, Sagittarius) are basically intuitive, energetic, and outgoing. The Earth signs (Taurus, Virgo, Capricorn) are practical, cautious, and patient. The mental realms are the home of the communicative Air signs (Gemini, Libra, Aquarius); while the Water signs (Cancer, Scorpio, Pisces) are primarily concerned with feelings.

The Sun signs are further divided into three groups; Cardinal, Fixed and Mutable. These are known as the 'triplicities'. Each group consists of four signs, one from each element. Each is concerned with a different way of operating in the world, So, the Cardinal signs (Aries, Cancer, Libra and Capricorn) are said to be ambitious initiators, leaders, and catalysts. The next zodiac group are known as the Fixed signs – Taurus, Leo, Scorpio and Aquarius. This indicates a resistance to change, an ability to conserve what has been initiated by the Cardinal group, plus a talent for seeing things through. Finally, the Mutable signs (Gemini, Virgo, Sagittarius and Pisces) contain versatile, fluid types who embody the principle of adaptability.

By combining element and triplicity, astrologers begin to build up a basic picture of someone's astrological make-up. For example, Aries, Leo and Sagittarius are Fire signs. But they express their fundamentally fiery vitality in different ways. Aries

The Moon, archetypally feminine, rules the sign of Cancer and has always been associated with the tides of the sea. (*De Sphaera* manuscript, fifteenth century)

typically likes to be the leader, a Cardinal attribute. Fixed Leo has great energy, but is slow to change, while fluid, Mutable Sagittarians use their energy in unexpected and sometimes erratic ways.

Sun sign astrology is the basis of all popular newspaper and magazine columns. It is, necessarily, generalized for it divides the whole population into twelve groups. However, it does form the basis of complex, personal astrology which requires an accurate horoscope, drawn up for the precise time and place of birth.

According to ancient magical lore, each sign reflects the prevailing mood of the cosmos at that particular moment in time; 'As above, so below'. Which part of the pattern are you? Learning about your Sun sign can be both enlightening and entertaining – you are certain to recognize at least something of yourself somewhere in the pages that follow.

Whatever is born or done this moment of time,
has the qualities of this moment of time.

Dr. CARL JUNG
Psychiatrist and psychoanalyst

Jupiter, Father of the Gods. The principles of Jupiter are expansion and optimism and this image illustrates his natural association with merchants and traders. (*De Sphaera* manuscript, fifteenth century)

— THE —
PLATES

PLATE I
ARIES, THE RAM
21st March–20th April

Cardinal Fire

Ruling Planet: Mars

KEYWORDS
Energetic; Active; Self-willed

Born under the first sign of the zodiac, Ariens are assertive, extrovert characters. Their ruling planet, Mars, was traditionally the planet of war: today, it signifies action and energy. These qualities permeate the typical Aries' nature, giving them what is perhaps the most single-minded sense of purpose in the entire zodiac. Their fearless honesty and pioneering spirit are always eager to rise to a challenge, or initiate fresh and innovative schemes. Notably restless, Aries' impatience can lead to over-impulsive actions.

The Arien's most negative characteristics are selfishness, aggression and an argumentative nature. Although this sign is linked with action, Ariens will procrastinate over life's mundane details, for they are happiest with broad views and large, inspiring concepts. At their most positive, they are dynamic achievers who long for, and generally get, adventure.

SOME ARIES CELEBRITIES: Sir Alec Guinness; Bette Davis; John Major; Lucrezia Borgia; Leonardo da Vinci; Diana Ross; Elton John; Warren Beatty

ARIES IN LOVE

Ariens are blessed with strong personalities, and an urge to dominate others. They are reckless romantics whose passionate temperament is rarely fulfilled by the single life. Both sexes are capable of ardent, romantic pursuit – for once Aries decides he or she wants someone, they rarely pause to think it through. And despite their tough exterior, they are surprisingly sensitive souls. Optimistic and idealistic, they are often disappointed in love for they place their partner on a pedestal.

In long-term partnerships, Aries men and women are loyal and affectionate. Lack of attention or excitement could prompt them to stray, however, for Aries lives life in the fast lane and cannot take unrelieved domesticity for ever. Their tendency to take the reins and dominate their partner can result in clashes of will and spectacular arguments. But since they rarely bear a grudge, this simply adds a sense of necessary drama to their love lives.

COMPATIBLE SIGNS: Gemini; Leo; Libra; Sagittarius

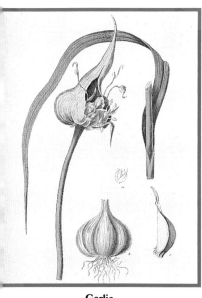

Garlic

Soldier

ARIES

COLOUR: Scarlet

GEM: Garnet

METAL: Iron

PLANTS:
Basil, garlic, onions, honeysuckle

PLACES:
England, Germany, Florence, Marseilles

ACTIVITIES / OCCUPATIONS:
Soldier, explorer, fireman, metalworker, blacksmith,
rally driver, community leader, mountaineer

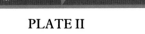

PLATE II
TAURUS, THE BULL
21 April–21 May

Fixed Earth

Ruling Planet: Venus

KEYWORDS
Patient; Sensuous; Enduring

Taurus the Bull is, above all, supremely stoical. Those born under his sign have steadfast natures and are primarily concerned with stability, security, and material comfort. Their patient pursuit of these aims often brings them lasting success in business. Taureans like to protect and conserve what they have achieved. Their characteristic attention to detail, and ability to see things through make them ideal partners for the more volatile signs.

Venus-ruled, Taureans are sensuous and tac-tile. Their sensible, reliable persona masks a sensitive soul who appreciates beauty. Taureans typically make wonderful cooks and talented artists. Proud of their homes, they will spend time and money creating ravishing gardens to set them off. Their astrological affinity with the earth is a powerful one, leading many of them to become involved with environmental and conservation issues. Negative Taurean characteristics are stubborness, resistance to change and a curious, irrational fear of spontaneity.

SOME TAURUS CELEBRITIES: HM Queen Elizabeth II; Sigmund Freud; Fred Astaire; Barbra Streisand; Glenda Jackson; Yehudi Menuhin; Audrey Hepburn; Orson Welles

TAURUS IN LOVE

Linked to Venus, planet of love, Taureans have romantic natures. Their sensual sexuality, coupled with a lazy charm makes them attractive to the opposite sex. However, driven as they are by a need for security, they dislike taking romantic risks. Their courtship is cautious; they will spend a long time getting to know someone before making their minds up. Ultimately, the Taurean seeks a partner with whom he or she can share their home and heart on a long-term basis. They do not require constant stimulation, but cherish the idea of loving companionship.

In marriage, or other committed relationship, Taureans make loyal, loving partners. Faithful and steadfast, they are too security-conscious and lazy to be disloyal. Their jealous, possessive temperaments can spoil relationships, however, for Taureans are often attracted by lively, flirtatious types who find their attitude overwhelming.

COMPATIBLE SIGNS: Pisces; Cancer; Taurus; Capricorn

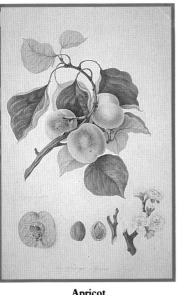

Apricot

Banker

TAURUS

COLOUR: Blue

GEM: Diamond

METAL: Copper

PLANTS:
Apricot tree, lily, violet, thyme

PLACES:
Iran, Iraq, Ireland, Lucerne, St Louis

ACTIVITIES / OCCUPATIONS:
Artist, jeweller, gardener, chef, singer, banker, accountant,
builder, dealer in art, antiques or property

PLATE III
GEMINI, THE TWINS
22 May–21 June

Mutable Air

Ruling Planet: Mercury

KEYWORDS
Communicative; Quick-witted; Inconsistent

Adaptable Gemini is the first Air sign of the zodiac. Geminis are, above all, restless and inquisitive, forever seeking mental stimulation. Their quest for knowledge is wide-ranging, for their curiosity about life is rarely satisfied. Ruled by Mercury, the messenger of the gods, they are superb communicators whose ability to broadcast their ideas through writing or speech is one of their great strengths.

Geminis require plenty of change in their daily lives. Without it, they become depressed and nervous, but rarely stay in this state for long. A dual sign, their nature is traditionally double-sided – one twin representing the witty, charming optimist, the other bleak, morose, and pessimistic. This, along with their inability to follow things through, represents their most negative trait. Mercury was also the god of liars; the Geminian facility for language has produced some talented dissemblers.

SOME GEMINI CELEBRITIES: John F. Kennedy; Bob Dylan; Judy Garland; Robert Maxwell; Isadora Duncan; Marilyn Monroe; Paul McCartney

GEMINI IN LOVE

Fickle and flirtatious, Geminis make playful, attractive lovers. They collect many admirers along the way, but find it difficult to sustain deep emotion. Social creatures, they resent anyone who tries to tie them down to a life of routine domesticity. Their ideal partner is entertaining and witty, with an absorbing life or career of their own.

Marriage and commitment are difficult for the typical Gemini, for their emotions are as changeable as their moods. With an undemanding partner they will usually remain faithful, but are notoriously prone to 'second strings' and double lives. Fearing emptiness, they will often marry more than once in an attempt to earth themselves. However happy they are with a partner, they often remain lifelong flirts and free spirits

COMPATIBLE SIGNS: Aries; Libra; Leo; Aquarius

Mandrake, supposed to cure every wound

Teacher

GEMINI

COLOUR: Bright yellow

GEM: Tiger's eye agate

METAL: Mercury

PLANTS:
Dill, lavender, mandrake, hogweed

PLACES:
Belgium, Wales, London, San Francisco

ACTIVITIES / OCCUPATIONS:
Journalist, broadcaster, linguist, postman, salesman,
teacher, travel agent, navigator, telephone operator

PLATE IV
CANCER, THE CRAB
22 June–22 July

Cardinal Water

Ruling Planet: The Moon

KEYWORDS
Tenacious; Intuitive; Protective

Cancerians are ruled by the ever-changing Moon, and this gives a crucial clue to their character. For, although they are tenacious and apparently self-assured, their moods fluctuate like the tides of the sea. Profoundly emotional and sensitive, they have finely-tuned psychic antennae and are extremely receptive. This awareness, coupled with outstanding memory, makes them shrewd and effective in their careers.

Cancerians are often ambitious, but their capacity for approaching every goal in a sideways manner may obscure this trait. Once they have achieved something, they will defend it with considerable strength and cunning. They make great collectors, and are typically drawn to antiques and silver. Cancerians' sense of history and family is often marked; they are drawn to 'family' type groups and organizations, and usually maintain close ties with their own flesh and blood, especially their mothers. Their most negative traits are moodiness, defensiveness and a tendency to harbour grudges.

SOME CANCER CELEBRITIES: Julius Caesar; Meryl Streep; George Orwell; Barbara Cartland; Ringo Starr; Emily Pankhurst; Modigliani

CANCER IN LOVE

Touchy and vulnersble, Cancerians of both sexes make emotional, but loving partners. Their tough shells cradle a soft interior world, full of sentiment and sensuality, However, their self-protective instincts are powerful; slights or disagreements result in a swift withdrawal beneath their significant defences. Inner turmoil is effectively hidden from potential partners, who may mistakenly believe the Cancerian to be cold and unfeeling. Nothing could be further from the truth about those born under this sign.

Commitment suits the Cancerian, who seeks security above all things. Cancer women are naturally maternal and usually long to have children. Failing this, they will care for the underdog or those in need. Cancer men make difficult partners, but are affectionate, loyal and protective once they have learned to overcome insecurity and trust their instincts.

COMPATIBLE SIGNS: Taurus; Virgo; Capricorn; Scorpio

Sailor

Mushrooms

CANCER

COLOUR: Silvery blue

GEM: Moonstone, pearl

METAL: Silver

PLANTS:
Lettuce, mushroom, pumpkin, white roses

PLACES:
Holland, New Zealand, Scotland, Milan,
New York, Venice

ACTIVITIES / OCCUPATIONS:
Catering, historian, hotelier, nurse, sailor,
tailor, antique dealer, publican, midwife

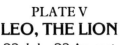

PLATE V
LEO, THE LION
23 July–23 August

Fixed Fire

Ruling Planet: The Sun

KEYWORDS
Dramatic; Enthusiastic; Generous

Sunny-natured extroverts, Leos are creative personalities whose purpose in life is to express themselves. Born leaders, they have a great sense of pride in themselves and their achievements, which can tip over into overbearing arrogance in its negative expression. Masters of the grand plan, Leos paint on a large canvas in life. They despise pettiness in all its forms, and are generally very extravagant with time, money, energy and love.

Leonine faults resemble those of a spoiled child, for Leos are frequently very child-like people. They can be loud and boastful, tactless, and stubbornly convinced that they, and they alone, are right. Their need for power may lead them to dominate others, or harbour overwhelming ambitions. However, Leo's generosity of spirit and unswerving principles make up for a lot. They are excellent organizers, and need plenty of love and encouragement.

SOME LEO CELEBRITIES: Princess Anne; Yves St Laurent; Mick Jagger; Fidel Castro; Jaqueline Kennedy Onassis; Napoleon Bonaparte; Percy Bysshe Shelley; Enid Blyton

LEO IN LOVE

Leos are the greatest romantics in the zodiac. Their feelings are intense, sincere, and passionate, and they fall in love at the drop of a hat. They adore dramatic gestures, and will shower their partner with presents, cards, and spontaneous surprises. Highly sexed, they wither and grow depressed without love. But prompted by their urgent desire for love, they may fall for several unsuitable partners before the right one comes along to mend their broken dreams.

Leos like being married, or in a committed relationship. They are extremely loyal, but their flirtatious natures could cause sparks to fly. The Leo tendency towards fixed opinions and autocratic behaviour may create marital mayhem, too. Leos are tempted to be unfaithful when their partner fails to praise them, or they feel unloved. When happily settled, Leos make entertaining, warm partners with large and generous hearts.

COMPATIBLE SIGNS: Aries; Libra; Sagittarius; Gemini

**Gold – crown of the kings of Prussia
stripped of its jewels**

Rosemary

LEO

COLOUR: Gold

GEM: Amber, ruby

METAL: Gold

PLANTS:
Almond, frankincense, rosemary,
marigold, sunflower

PLACES:
France, Italy, Bath, Los Angeles, Rome, Prague

ACTIVITIES / OCCUPATIONS:
Acting, astrologer, teacher, public relations executive,
entrepreneur, charity organiser, athlete, sculptor

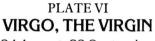

PLATE VI
VIRGO, THE VIRGIN
24 August–23 September

Mutable Earth

Ruling Planet: Mercury

KEYWORDS
Modest; Analytical; Discriminating

Virgo is a complex sign, for it is earthy and practical and yet able to adapt to changing circumstances. Virgoans possess a quick, analytical intelligence which is often hidden behind a reserved exterior. Their quiet charm and perceptive wit are revealed on closer acquaintance, while their subtle logic serves them well at work.

Virgoans are famed for their finely-honed critical faculties. These represent something of a double-edged sword, for they can be turned to destructive account with the greatest of ease. Although they are earthy by element, Virgoans are typically at home in the mental realms. This conflict between sensation and intellect inclines them to worry, suppress their emotions and undervalue their abilities. They are often hypochondriacs, and typically maintain high standards of hygiene and health care for themselves.

SOME VIRGO CELEBRITIES: Confucius; Goethe; Agatha Christie; Greta Garbo; Sean Connery; Sophia Loren; Ingrid Bergman; Ivan the Terrible

VIRGO IN LOVE

Virgoans are modest, conventional and refined in matters of love. Their affection is slow to grow, and they are rarely swept off their feet by a mysterious stranger. But Virgo is ruled by Mercury, and from time to time Virgoans reveal another, darker, side to their natures. Paradoxically, they can be as fickle and promiscuous in love as any Gemini. This is because they are able to detach themselves from their emotions, and take a purely rational view of love and sex.

Their impulse to serve others is usually marked, and once deeply involved Virgoans make loyal, loving partners. However, they do not crave companionship and are usually very self-sufficient singles. Their tendency to criticize and seek impossible perfection can undermine their relationships, but they are conscientious towards loved ones and rarely stray.

COMPATIBLE SIGNS: Virgo; Capricorn; Cancer; Taurus

Policeman

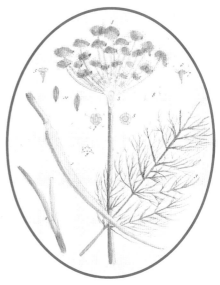

Fennel

VIRGO

COLOURS: Grey, navy

GEM: Sardonyx

METAL: Mercury

PLANTS:
Lily of the valley, sage, fennel, hazel, valerian

PLACES:
Greece, Turkey, Switzerland, Paris, Basle; Jerusalem

ACTIVITIES / OCCUPATIONS:
Dentist, doctor, tax inspector, teacher, secretary, writer,
editor, policeman / woman, cleaner, statistician, linguist

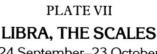

PLATE VII
LIBRA, THE SCALES
24 September–23 October

Cardinal Air

Ruling Planet: Venus

KEYWORDS
Balance; Unity; Diplomatic

Libra's symbolic scales were allocated to this sign by Babylonian astrologers, for at this time of year their gods weighed all things in the celestial scales, and decided upon the fates of mortals. Librans are continuing an ancient tradition when they struggle to make up their minds, a daily occurrence for this sign.

Self-expressive and communicative. Librans work best in a team. Their tact, charm and diplomacy bring them popularity and they usually lead active social lives. Librans delight in harmony, beauty, art and music. They dislike being alone, and will go to great lengths to create a peaceful welcoming atmosphere at home and at work. Beneath that lazy, effortless charm, they are often ambitious and self-willed – with a determination to succeed in their chosen field that mirrors their opposite sign, Aries. Their negative qualities are superficiality, indecisiveness, and untidiness.

SOME LIBRAN CELEBRITIES: John Lennon Margaret Thatcher; Aleister Crowley; T.S. Elliot; Brigitte Bardot; Luciano Pavarotti; Franz Liszt; John Lennon; Sarah Bernhardt

LIBRA IN LOVE

Libra is the sign of partnership. Librans' astrological impulse is to seek harmonious relationships with others, in friendship, business and above all in love. They are romantic, sentimental, and wonderfully flirtatious types who can make others feel extra special. Often physically attractive, with dazzling smiles, they are rarely without an admirer or two. Like Leo, Librans are in love with love. Unlike Leo, their approach is less passionate and more concerned with the marriage of true minds.

For all their drive towards relationships, Librans are often married more than once. Their natural flirtatiousness incites more jealous types to become argumentative and possessive. Since Librans abhor fights, such scenes may eventually prompt them to leave. With an undemanding, supportive partner, however, they are very happy with commitment.

COMPATIBLE SIGNS: Gemini; Leo; Aries; Libra

Rose

LIBRA

COLOURS: Light blue, pink

GEM: Emerald

METAL: Copper

PLANTS:
Daffodil, daisy, rose, foxglove, mint, parsley

PLACES:
Austria, Burma, Canada, Egypt, Copenhagen,
Lisbon, Vienna

ACTIVITIES / OCCUPATIONS:
Beautician, judge, designer, personnel officer,
dancer, florist, barrister, receptionist, landscape
gardener

PLATE VIII

SCORPIO, THE SCORPION

24 October–22 November

Fixed Water

Ruling Planets: Mars and Pluto

KEYWORDS
Secretive; Intense; Penetrating

Scorpio is generally defined as the most mysterious sign in the zodiac. Cloaked in enigma. Scorpions are instinctively self-protective and innately secretive. Others rarely know what Scorpio is thinking, while Scorpions pride themselves on their penetrating, intuitive insights. Scorpio's astrological impulse is to delve, to seek for hidden meaning, to uncover what is obscure. Natural detectives, they are often blessed with an uncanny sixth sense.

Scorpions make loyal friends, but are notoriously slow to take anyone into their confidence. Although their vitality is considerable, they resent scattering it socially. They tend towards introversion, and are happy spending time alone. Indeed, like their fellow Water signs, some private time is essential to restore their creativity and emotional equilibrium. Scorpio faults are somewhat dramatic; they can be breathtakingly vindictive, jealous, and resentful – the saying 'revenge is a dish that is best served cold' was probably coined by a Scorpion.

SOME SCORPION CELEBRITIES: Bram Stoker Richard Burton; Martin Luther; Pablo Picasso; Katherine Hepburn; Joan Sutherland

SCORPIO IN LOVE

Powerful and passionate, Scorpion feelings run deep. Once in love, they focus single-mindedly upon the object of desire, for in their subtle way they aim to win this person's love for ever. Scorpio rules the genitals and traditionally they are said to possess strong libidos and urgent desires. However, on the negative side Scorpions can be self-repressive, an ice-cap atop a smouldering volcano.

Scorpions prefer long-term relationships which allow them to explore intimacy. Characteristically compulsive and obsessive, their emotional nature requires commitment if it is to blossom. They do not relinquish love easily, preferring fight to flight, and battling to maintain any relationship they believe to be worthwhile. Jealousy, coupled with suspicion, may prove hard for partners to cope with. Unhappiness can act as a catalyst for infidelity; when unfaithful, Scorpions are capable of intricate deceptions worthy of a professional spy.

COMPATIBLE SIGNS: Cancer; Scorpio; Capricorn; Pisces

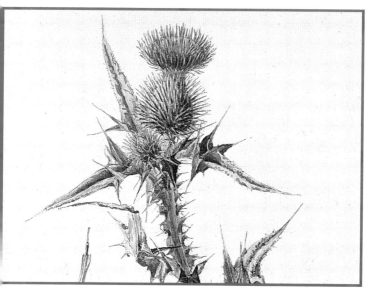

Thistle

SCORPIO

COLOURS: Deep red, black

GEM: Opal

METAL: Steel

PLANTS:
Cactus, ginger, broom, briar, thistles,
horseradish, ginseng

PLACES:
Algeria, Morocco, Liverpool, New Orleans,
Norway, Syria

ACTIVITIES / OCCUPATIONS:
Butcher, chemist, detective, psychologist,
researcher, magician, undertaker, archaeologist,
sex therapist, occultist

PLATE IX

SAGITTARIUS, THE ARCHER

23 November–21 December

Mutable Fire

Ruling Planet: Jupiter

KEYWORDS
Adventurous; Philosophical; Expansive

Ebullient, humorous Sagittarians are the explorers af the zodiac. Many of them travel extensively throughout their lives, while others investigate mental dimensions – studying philosophy, politics, psychology or law. Essentially, they seek to expand their horizons mentally and physically – and require the freedom to do so.

Symbolically half man, half horse, many Sagittarians are attracted by an open-air life. They have a close affinity with nature and an innate understanding of animals – particularly horses and dogs. Active sports, such as running or riding, provide an ideal outlet for their restless vitality. Their mental agility and open-minded attitudes win them many friends, and they generally enjoy a wide, sometimes eccentric, range of acquaintances. Anyone close to a Sagittarian should have a thick skin, for they are noted for their tactlessness. Supreme optimists, Sagittarians rarely reveal their darker side to anyone. A tendency to depression and an ability for inflated thinking, can cast shadows across their sunny temperaments.

SOME SAGITTARIAN CELEBRITIES: Woody Allen; Beethoven; Jane Austen; Nostradamus; Jane Fonda; Sir Winston Churchill; Maria Callas

THE SAGITTARIAN IN LOVE

Ardent, yet changeable, the Sagittarian typically finds it difficult to settle down. Although fiery, warm and passionate, this is a Mutable sign – which gives a mercurial twist to the personality. Extravagant and expansive, the Sagittarian may sweep someone off their feet – only suddenly to change their mind, leaving a bewildered partner behind. Conventional commitment can be a difficult step for Sagittarians, for their curiosity about the opposite sex is rarely satisfied by one person.

Fresh air and freedom beckon every Sagittarian sooner or later. A wise partner will accommodate this need, and allow their beloved space and a stumulating social life. Sagittarians dislike arguments, and abhor jealous scenes. They are loyal in love, and extremely affectionate – so long as they do not feel fenced in. Should this happen, they are more likely to leave than engage in a series of affairs.

COMPATIBLE SIGNS: Aries; Aquarius; Leo; Libra

Priest

Almond

SAGITTARIUS

COLOURS: Indigo, purple

GEM: Topaz

METAL: Tin

PLANTS:
Almond, borage, cloves, myrrh, chervil,
mint, rhubarb

PLACES:
Australia, Hungary, Spain, Naples,
Cologne, Budapest

ACTIVITIES / OCCUPATIONS:
Bookseller, showjumper, jockey, lawyer,
teacher, travel agent, vet, writer, explorer,
interpreter, priest, philosopher, librarian

PLATE X
CAPRICORN, THE FISH-TAILED GOAT

22 December–20 January

Cardinal Earth

Ruling Planet: Saturn

KEYWORDS
Discipline; Resourcefulness; Caution

Ancient Roman astrologers claimed that the soul incarnated in Cancer, and learned the last of its spiritual lessons in Capricorn. The Chaldeans linked it with the fish-tailed goat, Capricornus, who brought culture and civilization to the world. Traditionally destined to think deeply and rationally, Capricorns are typically self-disciplined and stoical. Responsible and conscientious, they are nonetheless ambitious – especially when it comes to achieving material security.

Capricorns make steady progress in life, generally achieving their goals eventually. Bereft of a sense of purpose, they become withdrawn and pessimistic. Strangely enough, for such a cautious and prudent sign, they are prone to occasional bouts of extravagance for they are fond of fine things. An ironic sense of humour serves to lighten their typically reserved personalities. However, their strong sense of duty invariably prevails. Critical and exacting, Capricorns are prone to worry unneccessarily and dislike taking risks.

SOME CAPRICORN CELEBRITIES: Humphrey Bogart; Paul Cézanne; Marlene Deitrich; Louis Pasteur; Puccini; Anthony Hopkins; Faye Dunaway

CAPRICORN IN LOVE

Ruled by Saturn, planet of boundaries and restrictions, Capricorns take a serious view of true love. They make poor flirts, but outstandingly loyal and loving long-term partners. Although traditionally said to be dour and emotionally repressed, Capricorn is also a sensuous, earthy sign. Beneath that cautious, serious exterior they can be profoundly sentimental and romantic. Like their opposite sign, Cancer, they find it difficult to express their emotions and appear cool and unfeeling to more open, volatile types.

Capricorns seek security in their emotional dealings with others. And it takes them a long time to trust someone enough to reveal their love. Characteristically, this is a prelude to conventional commitment. Faithful and true, Capricorns work hard to establish a solid marriage. If disappointed in love, they rarely show their distress – but fight shy of fresh involvement for a very long time.

COMPATIBLE SIGNS: Cancer; Taurus; Virgo; Scorpio

Farming

CAPRICORN

COLOURS: Dark brown, grey

GEM: Jet

METAL: Lead

PLANTS:
Barley, beech, deadly nightshade, holly, ivy,
willow, yew, comfrey

PLACES:
Afghanistan, Bulgaria, India, Mexico,
Brussels, Oxford

ACTIVITIES / OCCUPATIONS:
Architect, builder, farmer, musician, scientist,
surveyor, prison warder, bank manager,
stockbroker, wine merchant, politician

PLATE XI

AQUARIUS, THE WATER BEARER

21 January–19 February

Fixed Air

Ruling Planets: Saturn and Uranus

KEYWORDS
Progressive; Humanitarian; Inventive

Energetic and quick-witted, the typical Aquarian is independent, idealistic and progressive. Their humanitarian leanings attract them to causes, whether political or spiritual – many Aquarians espouse unconventional beliefs in these areas. Great explorers, they love to investigate the unusual and are often notably avant-garde thinkers.

This sign comes under the dominion of both Saturn and Uranus. Saturn gives Aquarians staying power, and a certain dogmatic intensity. Uranus, planet of revolution and upheaval, inspires their unpredictable visions and rebellious phases. Aquarians identify themselves with the community, the brotherhood of man, with progression and reform. Detached and inventive, Aquarians can become erratic and self-centred. Their tactlessness may provoke rifts in friendships, or alienate colleagues. However, they typically maintain a wide circle of friends, while their enthusiasm and child-like curiosity is most appealing.

SOME AQUARIAN CELEBRITIES: Galileo; Lord Byron; Placido Domingo; Jeanne Moreau; Collette; Germaine Greer; Paul Newman; Vanessa Redgrave

AQUARIUS IN LOVE

As curious about love as everything else, Aquarians take a somewhat dispassionate view of emotional attachments. Their charm and wit can be most captivating, but is generally intended to be friendly rather than seductive. Passionately involved with the whole of humanity, the Aquarian characteristically finds intimate, one-to-one relationships difficult. Mental rapport and stimulation are essential to any Aquarian liaison, as is a good deal of personal space.

However, despite their fierce independence, Aquarians enjoy team-work. Ideally, this leads to a relationship where both partners share in fighting for a cause, or other intellectual pursuits. Their innate loyalty is sometimes in conflict with their need for freedom. This, combined with their erratic tendencies, can make for unconventional relationships. An emotionally demanding partner is not a happy match for Aquarius, who can become cool and detached when confronted with another's individual needs.

COMPATIBLE SIGNS: Aquarius; Sagittarius; Gemini

Astronomer

AQUARIUS

COLOURS: Electric blue, silver grey

GEM: Aquamarine

METAL: Platinum

PLANTS:
Pansy, moss, pine, quince, sorrel, spinach,
snowdrops, parsnip

PLACES:
Poland, Sweden, Russia, Hamburg, Moscow

ACTIVITIES / OCCUPATIONS:
Astrologer, broadcaster, computer programmer,
pilot, electrician, inventor, sociologist, social
worker, pilot, astronomer, physicist

PLATE XII

PISCES, THE FISHES

20 February–20 March

Mutable Water

Ruling Planets: Jupiter and Neptune

KEYWORDS
Sensitive; Imaginative; Flexible

As the last sign of the zodiac, Pisces is said to contain aspects of every other sign within its complex nature. Synthesizing the lessons of the previous eleven types is Pisces' spiritual task. Profoundly sensitive, and often psychic, Pisceans are ruled by expansive Jupiter, and dreamy Neptune. Typically, they are artistic, impressionable, and fluid. When positively channelled, their adaptability allows them to come up with outstandingly creative solutions to problems. When negatively expressed, this trait manifests in vacillation and duality.

Seeking to transcend the material world, Pisceans may become lost in visionary dreams and fail to achieve anything in this world. Gifted mimics and actors, they hide behind a mask, shielding themselves from the harsh realities of life. They are extremely receptive to atmospheres, and empathize with others in a truly compassionate manner. This response to others' suffering may lead them to become involved with voluntary work, charities or caring professions.

SOME PISCEAN CELEBRITIES: Michael Caine; Frederic Chopin; Elizabeth Taylor; Pierre-August Renoir; Liza Minnelli; Albert Einstein

PISCES IN LOVE

Overflowing with emotion, the Piscean drifts in an out of romantic dreams in a charactertistic search for ecstasy. A Mutable sign, they can be fickle, switching their emotional focus rapidly and without warning. Since they are flirtatious and seductive, they often leave a trail of broken hearts in their wake. However, Pisces is a dependent sign. The Pisceans' need for love, affection and support is compelling, and they are rarely content to be alone for long.

Pisceans long for spiritual union. They dream of bliss, of the ideal and perfect partner, of true love. This may lead them to marry more than once, for as incurable romantics, they firmly believe in fairy-tale endings. Deeply wounded by disappointment, they nevertheless are capable of complete recovery and rarely become bitter or cautious. Their deep desire for love is such that they will readily risk everything again and again in their search for lasting happiness.

COMPATIBLE SIGNS: Scorpio; Taurus

Water Lily

PISCES

COLOURS: Lilac, sea green

GEM: Bloodstone

METAL: Zinc

PLANTS:
Balm, chestnut, seaweed, water lily, dandelion, aniseed, nutmeg

PLACES:
Portugal, Tanzania, Tonga, Alexandria, Seville

ACTIVITIES / OCCUPATIONS:
Artist, chiropodist, poet, photographer, fishmonger, healer, hospital worker, publican, visionary, film director, swimming-pool attendant; psychic

PICTURE ACKNOWLEDGEMENTS

INTRODUCTION
Frontispiece: British Library, London; Imprint page –
Capricorn, E T Archive/Glasgow University Library;
Anatomy of Man and Woman, Bridgeman Art Library/
Giraudon/Musée Condé, Chantilly; Jupiter and Moon,
E T Archive/Biblioteca Estense, Modena; The Celestial Sky,
Studio Editions Ltd.

PLATES
Bridgeman Art Library: Details of sun-signs from a Book of
Hours by the Fastolf Master, fifteenth century, Bodleian
Library, Oxford. The shelfmark for this volume is Ms
Auct.D.inf.2.II, folio numbers are listed after each entry:-
Aries f.3r; Taurus f.4r; Gemini f.5r; Cancer f.6r; Leo f.7r;
Virgo f.8r; Libra f.9r; Scorpio f.10r; Sagittarius f.11r;
Capricorn f.12r; Aquarius f.1r; Pisces f.2r. Gold Crown,
Schloss Charlottenburg, Berlin; Thistle, Victoria & Albert
Museum, London; Farming, from Book of Hours of the
Blessed Virgin, British Library, London; Waterlily, Royal
Botanical Gardens, Kew.

E T Archive: Garlic; Apricot, Royal Horticultural Society;
Banker; Mandrake; Sailor, National Maritime Museum;
Rosemary; Fennel; Almond; Astronomer.

Image Select: Mushrooms.

Studio Editions Ltd: Soldier; Teacher; Policeman; White
Rose; Priest.